MW00399714

EVERYTHING
THAT MAKES YOU
Mom

EVERYTHING
THAT MAKES YOU

A BOUQUET
OF MEMORIES

LAURA LYNN BROWN

Abingdon Press / Nashville

EVERYTHING
THAT MAKES YOU *Mom*
A BOUQUET OF MEMORIES

This book is printed on acid-free paper.

ISBN 978-1-4267-6746-3

13 14 15 16 17 18 19 20 21 22—10 9 8 7 6 5 4 3 2 1
MANUFACTURED IN THE UNITED STATES OF AMERICA

Contents

INTRODUCTION

Word to the Mothers

See, we have been paying attention.

All those years of advice, of your words of wisdom, of loving, of scolding, of shaping? We heard. And we remember.

You'll encounter two stories here. One is a collection of memories of my mother, who died before I was able to offer her such a bouquet. But there's still joy in the sharing of the remarkable woman she was, and in offering vignettes that might bear some resemblance to your own memories of mothering.

The larger story, though, is your own child's retelling of who you are as a mom. You'll notice that each set of pages offers a short list of questions to get those memories flowing, with that opening micro-essay as a starting point. Each question reflects some aspect I would have wanted to explore for and with my own mother. Using the space after the questions, your child, or both of you together, can fill in the gaps with the richness of your distinctive history.

Quotations throughout the book, about moms and from moms, have been chosen to provide commentary, spiritual insight, wisdom, and delight about the experiences of being and having a mother.

We're grown now, out making our way in the world, and that way is some reflection on your work as a mother. Were you successful?

I'll offer something that I found in my own mother's Bible, in her small, neat handwriting. No doubt she meant it in a larger context, but it applies to mothering too.

> Success—a progressive realization of a worthy goal.
>
> Principles for achieving our goal:

1. Put first things first
2. Be enthusiastic
3. Give a full measure and more
4. Work—be persistent—sacrifice.

In a way, this collection of memories is your child's testament to your success in raising a girl to be a woman, a boy to be a man.

There's not a book big enough to contain all that mothers have said and done and been for us. But my hope is that in its own way, in the words on the page and the memories evoked, this book will feel much larger than its size. Perhaps it will also reassure you that there are fresh seeds being planted, new blooms to be grown, in the changing and ongoing relationship between you and your child.

There's another handwritten list, in the back of my mother's Bible, under the heading "Responsibilities of Parenthood," and I can attest that she fulfilled them. Two lines especially stand out:

> Try to be as Christ-like as possible. Then we will become the kind of people who are good parents.
>
> Parenthood does not terminate. It goes on forever.

WHY NOW

You're probably receiving this for Mother's Day, the most obvious gift-giving occasion for moms. It's a good one. (Anna Jarvis, the ramrod behind the institution of Mother's Day, thought mere cards were lame. She advocated writing to mothers, as you will see later in these pages.) But Mother's Day isn't the only occasion. Maybe you're getting this for your birthday (and what a great way for your child to disobey you after you selflessly instructed, "Oh, don't get me anything").

Yet there are other special occasions when the element of surprise is part of the gift, because you *really* won't be expecting anything.

Maybe your child is about to leave the nest, or has recently flown. Consider this an accounting of gratitude for all those years of love and care and attention (and to show that those stubborn ears really were open during all the nudging and lecturing and teasing).

Maybe you are about to leave your nest for a smaller, later-in-life nest. Your grown child's recollections can help feather it with memories of places left behind.

Maybe your child is about to become a parent, and you're about to become a grandmother. Memories of all that you put into that work will shape the way the next generation carries it forth.

Maybe your kid wanted to commemorate something you've always done together—the lake vacation, the movie matinee, the garage sale shopping, the candlelight Christmas Eve service, the jam making, the ritual watching of the Miss America contest.

Last, but certainly not least, you might be getting this bouquet of memories for no reason at all, out of the same impulse that propelled a small child long ago to hand you a bouquet of milky dandelions just picked from the front yard: "Here. I see you. I love you. I know you."

Word to Gift-Giving Daughters and Sons

There's something about a mother's love that inspires gift giving. "Mama" is the first word some of us say, surely a gift to her ears. And she might have been the first person we gave something to, not for any occasion, but out of the desire to bestow something in the twin impulses of "I love you" and "I see you." Maybe it was abstract art in the medium of crayon, which she displayed on the gallery of the refrigerator door, hung low enough for the artist to appraise. Maybe it was a bunch of dandelions, relaxing in your hand on the trip between the yard and wherever she was.

This book invites you to give your mother another bouquet, a little more time-taking in the picking but longer-lasting and more varied than those drooping blooms of long-gone summers.

Maybe the woman you offered those blooms to did not carry you in the womb. There are stepmothers, adoptive mothers, foster mothers, neighborhood-it-takes-a-village mothers, and other kinds of mothers for whom there's no conventional terminology. So maybe yours didn't know you and feel you within before you were born. Maybe you could hold a conversation in complete sentences by the time you met her. But if you consider or call her Mom, then Mom she is to you, and this is for her too.

There are books that invite the users to interview their mothers, filling in the blanks and filling out a record of moments large and small in the mother's life. Questions are a good thing, and blessed is the grown child who wants to ask, and marvelous is the mother who enjoys answering. This book is different. Here, the questions are for you, the daughters and sons.

Take the time to wander through the gardens and greenhouses and fields and abandoned lots of memory. Maybe you'll even want to fill this in together with Mom, talking through each flower of the bouquet. There are questions here, and you get to consider them, and to surprise (not to mention delight, honor, gratify, regale, and cheer) Mom with your answers.

How to Use This Book

Each vignette begins with a recollection that is about my mom, but has a universal Momness to it, something that most people can identify with, or recognize, enhanced with their own experiences. These vignettes are followed by three questions or suggestions to help exercise your own memory muscles. The remaining space gives you room to write.

Those who like to follow the rules and those with ready recall (and perhaps those of us with many years of observing Mom to draw from) might answer every question. A gold star to each of you who can do that.

You don't have to answer every question, however. Maybe only one question from each trio will open your memory.

You might want to answer a question I haven't asked.

You might want to begin by making a list of mom stories.

You might even want to draw, or to tape in a photograph or a ticket stub or another memento, to add a visual component to some of your memories.

If you have siblings, this could be a collaborative project. Gather for a meal, pool your memories, and take turns writing after the dishes are cleared. Any accidental food stains will simply add flavor to your pages.

Consider this your permission slip to fill out and fill up this book in whatever way gives you joy.

THE POWER OF A STORY IN A SENTENCE

Remember when you learned to read? Probably it was Mom who sat next to you when you sounded out the syllables, then made them words, then began to package them in sentences, one at a time. A sentence can say enough to evoke a paragraph's worth of memory. Many of the vignettes here are a single sentence. Sometimes a single sentence is enough. Sometimes it is everything.

You may, of course, write in your tiniest handwriting and fill up all the space you have with long, detailed chains of sentences. But a sentence is often enough. My sentences will prompt you to fill in the space with your memories; your sentences will allow your mother to do the same.

Now, to that work (and play!). Most of this book is yet to be written. The little stories that begin the course are my own memories. These sentences, though, are just the ferns and baby's breath in this bouquet. Let your own sentences be the blooms.

Mom in the Home

There she is in the kitchen, cooking a birthday
dinner, making gravy with glee, upholding
holiday rituals, fighting grime.
And there she is on the porch, and in the yard,
doing whatever she did to make a house a
home that we loved to live in and would want
to return to, so naturally that we probably
didn't even notice.

Mom bought a gravy whisk that we saw in a specialty kitchen store not so much because she needed a gravy whisk, but because its packaging claimed, "It scoffs at lumps." She gave it a new name: lump scoffer. When she made gravy, she whisked with glee, scoffing at those lumps herself with a single "Ha!"

What kitchen tasks does she relish?

Does she have nicknames for any of her gadgets?

How was your mother persuaded by advertising?

Instantly I bolted into the next room to read it aloud to mother and sister, and we all cheered in unison when we came to the Rah! Rah! Rah! part of it. —Theodore Roosevelt

In her kitchen, a cookie jar occupied the central place that a coffeemaker would have in other kitchens. Her favorite store-bought were Keebler Pecan Sandies and Archway Date-filled Oatmeal. Her favorite homemade were date-nut pinwheels, one of a dozen kinds she would make at Christmas. She was a dunker —in tea, not coffee.

What sweet treats does your mother favor?

Coffee, tea, or something else?

What has a place of prominence in her kitchen?

A mother is a person who, seeing there are only four pieces of pie for five people, promptly announces she never did care for pie. —Tenneva Jordan

On my fifth birthday, when I was hoarding the party hats and noisemakers out of an existential crisis, she spoke to me and got me to willingly distribute them, not so much because of whatever she said—which I don't remember—but because of the gentle, quiet, respectful way she said it.

What's the best birthday party your mom arranged for you?

How did she handle a crisis in your childhood?

Was there a time when her gentleness won the day?

A mother understands what a child does not say.

—Jewish proverb

Early enough in my childhood that I don't really remember it, she taught me the classic pair of childhood prayers—for the table, "God is great, God is good, let us thank Him for our food," and for bedtime, "Now I lay me down to sleep, I pray the Lord my soul to keep. If I should die before I wake, I pray the Lord my soul to take." In effect, I see now, it was teaching reliance on God and a hope and expectation of heaven.

What prayers, or equivalents, did your mother teach you?

What are her prayers like, or do you even know?

How did she invite God into daily habits?

From my mother I learned the value of prayer, how to have dreams and believe I could make them come true.

—Ronald Reagan

The time I got so mad that I announced I was running away from home, she asked me to pause long enough that she could note what I was wearing, so she would know how to describe me to the police when she filed a missing persons report. I made it three houses away before my resolve melted, but went all the way around the block just to save face.

Did your mom ever deal with a fit by pretending to take you seriously?

How has she made it hard to stay mad?

Has she blessed your independence in ways that make you want to come home?

And I—I went back to the old home,
to Denmark and to my mother;
because I just couldn't stay away any longer.

—Jacob A. Riis

She deep-fried countless shrimp in years of fulfilling my perennial birthday dinner request, and when we came home from college, she always welcomed us back with vegetable beef soup for me and apple pie for my brother.

What favorite food requests has she fulfilled?

How has your mother shown love through food?

What do you hope for when you show up for dinner?

Life is the fruit she longs to hand you,...
Relentlessly she understands you.

—Phyllis McGinley

On the hottest days of summer, Mom would loop the garden hose over a maple tree branch in the yard and set the nozzle on continuous spray so we could run through a cooling shower in our swimsuits. And in an era long before Super Soakers, empty Joy bottles became our large-capacity squirt guns.

What kinds of water play did your mother encourage?

Does she practice recycling, or frugality by another name?

In what ways was she creative with common household objects?

Where there is a mother in the home,
matters go well.

—Amos Bronson Alcott

When I was in grade school, on the coldest winter mornings, the kind that would leave frost patterns and a layer of ice on the bedroom windows, she would heat the stove and open the oven door so I could get dressed in the kitchen's warmth.

How did your mom make things cozy?

When did she take the chill off for you?

What did she do to make her kitchen a welcoming place?

Anyone who doesn't miss the past
never had a mother.
—Gregory Nunn

Spring cleaning was concentrated in the kitchen, and meant pulling the appliances and free-standing storage out from the wall and cleaning everything from top to bottom and underneath, and exchanging the storm doors for screen doors, and it was always a time when Mom and Dad both worked hard (though his tasks were mostly at her direction) and displayed both complementary and complimentary teamwork.

What cleaning rituals has your mother endorsed?

Who did she enlist to help?

Are there chores that you're glad she made you do?

One of the very few reasons I had any respect for my mother when I was thirteen was because she would reach into the sink with her bare hands—bare hands—and pick up that lethal gunk and drop it into the garbage. To top that, I saw her reach into the wet garbage bag and fish around in there looking for a lost teaspoon. Bare hands—a kind of mad courage. —Robert Fulghum

The hardest I ever saw her laugh may have been the year two mice rode in on the Christmas tree. When one zipped into the kitchen, my sister-in-law pinned it with the dust mop; my brother (possibly fueled by the adrenaline of mouse-fear) seized the broom, and together they swept it out the back door—a different kind of marital cooperation. The laugh's sound has faded, but its character was boneless mirth.

What epic tales does your mother recall with hilarity?

How might she deal with animal intruders?

What does her laugh sound like?

I am sure that if the mothers of various nations could meet, there would be no more wars. —E. M. Forster

Mom relished an approaching thunderstorm and enjoyed sitting on the front porch, watching the neighbors' trees thrash, waiting to greet it, lightning and all. Because I wanted to be with her, I did too.

When did your mother display a great sense of anticipation?

How has she weathered storms?

Have you inherited any of her fearlessness?

When I stopped seeing my mother
with the eyes of a child, I saw the woman
who helped me give birth to myself.

—Nancy Friday

Mom in the World

She was our primary tour guide into the neighborhood, and then into the world of commerce, where she gave us our first lessons in choosing wisely from all the shiny things the world, or at least the five-and-dime, had to offer. Farther afield, there were family vacations. Some of our moms went into the world to work, and sometimes there, as at home, Mom fulfilled duties far outside the scope of the job description.

On summer evenings, the neighbor women who lived up and down Kennon Street would gather on Mrs. Menkemiller's porch, and when Mom went, I got to go too, which was probably the first situation in which I learned that I could stay up late if I just quietly sat and listened long enough that the adults seemed to forget I was there.

What neighbors did your mom visit with?

How did she initiate you into the rituals or the company of neighborly adulthood?

What have you picked up from simply listening?

The mother-child relationship is paradoxical and, in a sense, tragic. It requires the most intense love on the mother's side, yet this very love must help the child grow away from the mother, and to become fully independent. —Erich Fromm

She also liked to walk in the neighborhood on summer evenings, and would get me to join her by saying, "Let's go look in people's windows."

What simple pleasures did she invite you along on?

How did she show curiosity about people's inner lives?

How has she been a good neighbor?

Making a decision to have a child—it's momentous. It is to decide forever to have your heart go walking around outside your body.

—Elizabeth Stone

Mom denied it, but Dad said she went sledding on a steep hill with the neighborhood kids, pregnant with me, the winter I was born, and I teased her—"I remember, it was chilly and dark and we went *very* fast!"—because I wanted it to be true.

Do you remember playing winter sports with your mother?

What is something about your mother that you know only through someone else's storytelling?

What do you like to tease her about?

Life began with waking up
and loving my mother's face.

—George Eliot

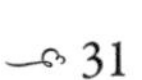

Mom was a human GPS, long before those units or MapQuest or the Internet was invented. She did all the navigating on trips, with a combination of maps, AAA Trip-tiks, verbal directions, visual observation, and spatial memory, and she never got us lost.

What kind of navigator is your mother?

Is she good at giving directions/what kind of directions has she given you when you went off course?

What places would her car feel its way to by habit?

Any mother could perform
the jobs of several air traffic
controllers with ease.

—Lisa Alther

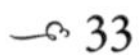

We rode the bus across the river into the city and made our rounds of places she liked to go (the Piece Goods fabric store, where I hated the smell of flocked fabric and learned to occupy myself flipping through the big books of patterns to the costumes section) and places I liked to go (Murphy's Five-and-Ten, where I sometimes could choose something small from two equally tantalizing sections: toys and office supplies).

What's a favorite store for your mother?

When you were bored, did she suggest an activity or let you figure something out on your own?

When did Mom require your patience, and how did she reward you for it?

Mama exhorted her children at every opportunity to "jump at de sun." We might not land on the sun, but at least we would get off the ground. —Zora Neale Hurston

On summer beach vacations, she loved Lingo's, the family-owned little corner grocery store where we bought the morning paper, and she christened some of the employees Bingo, Dingo, and Mingo Lingo.

When has your mother seemed most relaxed on vacation?

What are her vacation rituals?

Where would you like to take or send her on vacation?

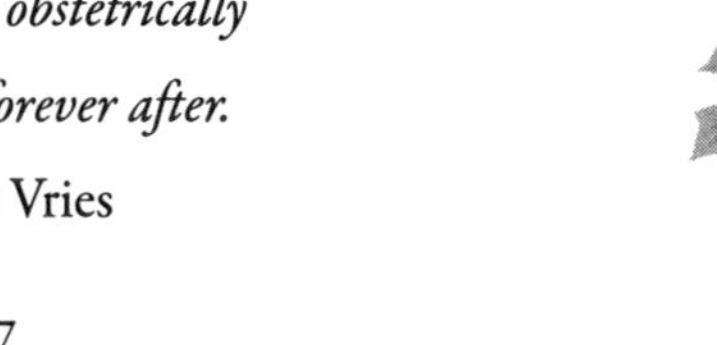

A suburban mother's role is to deliver children obstetrically once, and by car forever after.

—Peter De Vries

Mom didn't drive, so during the years when Dad worked on Sundays, she got us up and fed and ready to be picked up by the church van, where we rode with an assorted mix of people whom we might not have encountered otherwise, but with whom we felt some kinship, I think, simply because of our shared journey to a common destination.

What was your mom's role in your Sunday morning routines?

What obstacles of transportation has your mother overcome?

How, in word or deed, did she teach you to respect and value all kinds of people?

My mother had handed down respect for the possibilities... and the will to grasp them. —Alice Walker

We spent a week at Bethany Beach, Delaware, during the summer of Watergate, which Mom was fascinated by. She was certain she had seen John Dean walking the beach early one morning.

What news events have fascinated your mother?

Has she had any celebrity sightings?

How has she modeled a difference in public life and private life? Or is she the same everywhere, with everyone?

All that I am, or hope to be, I owe to my angel mother.

—Abraham Lincoln

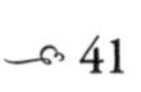

In her work-and-church-clothes wardrobe, Mom had several blouses she referred to as her Grace Van Owen blouses—the kind the *L.A. Law* character wore—silklike blouses with a rolled collar and a V-neck, and inside them, discreet safety pins to make the décolletage a centimeter or two more modest.

What are some of your mother's favorite dress-up clothes?

How did she display or advocate modesty?

Where has she employed safety pins?

When you are a mother, you are never really alone in your thoughts. A mother always has to think twice, once for herself and once for her child. —Sophia Loren

During the years she worked as a bank teller, she successfully lobbied to get the lunchroom moved out of the ladies' restroom.

What causes is your mother passionate about?

In what ways has her activism manifested itself?

How has she persuaded someone else to raise their standards?

When love is gone, there's always justice.
And when justice is gone, there's always force.
And when force is gone, there's always Mom.
Hi, Mom! —Laurie Anderson

Mom was an aide at my grade school, and when my young sixth grade teacher's husband died in a truck accident at work, Mom was the one to give her the news, not because she was the employee closest to Mrs. Kirk but because of her quiet strength in such times, and her grasp of what words to choose and how to deliver them.

When has your mother had to deliver bad news?

When has she had to receive bad news?

How is she at crisis management?

If you have a mom, there is nowhere you are likely to go where a prayer has not already been.

—Robert Brault

Virtuous Mom

Evidence of a mother's virtues is everywhere, once you start looking. Sometimes it's in her actions—reliability in a game of blind trust, tenderness in bandaging a wounded finger, foresight in planting a tree that will outlast her. And sometimes it's in the things she touches—respect written in a bookmark, thrift sewn into an action figure's shorts, forgiveness wrapped inside a purse.

Mom inherited land that had been owned by several generations of women, and she loved to "go out to the hill," to walk it and plan where she and Dad would build their retirement home. At the top of a long cleared field, she staked her claim by planting fruit trees.

What land is your mother most strongly associated with?

What plants has she tended?

What else has she planted that will outlast her?

She surveys a field and acquires it;
from her own resources,
she plants a vineyard.
—Proverbs 31:16

I was in college when I finally got too big for the trust exercise, which we always played in the kitchen. I would stand with my back to her, lean backwards, and when I began to lose my balance, she would catch me under my armpits before I hit the floor.

How does your mother demonstrate her trustworthiness?

Besides hugs and kisses, what are your other ritual forms of greeting?

How does she have your back?

A mother is not a person to lean on,

but a person to make leaning unnecessary.

—Dorothy Canfield Fisher

From my childhood through my teen years, mom sewed clothing for me, including a long denim duster; a purple ultrasuede vest with a sunrise appliquéd on the back in felt and with hippie fringe around the bottom; a Nehru jacket; a skirt and matching vest in a pastel floral fabric, which became my performance outfit for flute competitions; and my favorite, a winter-worthy poncho she made me in second grade, wide-wale corduroy in school bus orange on the outside, thick plush fake fur in pumpkin orange on the inside, closed at the neck with the kind of metal hooks on a fireman's jacket, fringed around the bottom with Mexican hat balls.

What did your mother dress you in?

What was a favorite garment or outfit from your childhood?

Did she allow unusual combinations that adults couldn't get away with (or herself wear unusual combinations)?

Sweater, n.: *garment worn by child when its mother is feeling chilly.* —Ambrose Bierce

Mom turned some fabric scraps into doll clothes, devising the patterns herself. My Barbie got some new outfits with tiny snaps or teeny hooks and eyelets; my favorite was a burnt orange floor-length cape with little slits for her hands. A red cotton print with small white flowers provided my brother's G.I. Joe with an open-chested Hawaiian shirt and matching board shorts.

What did your mother do with scraps (any kind of scraps)?

Did she make accessories for your playthings?

How did she fashion a sense of humor?

Who is getting more pleasure from this rocking, the baby or me?

—Nancy Thayer

For a PTA auction, Mom sewed and stuffed a two-foot-long hippo with plush fur, a rickrack tutu skirt, a rosebud mouth, and coy eyelashes. Dad valued the work she put into it so much that he couldn't bear to see someone else take it home, so he won it back—and for a good price, too, because for a while he and Mom were accidentally bidding against each other.

Was your mother involved in the PTA or other forms of school boosterism?

What finished products did she take pride in?

Did your parents ever accidentally work against each other toward the same goal?

Let her share in the results
of her work;
let her deeds praise her in the city gates.
—Proverbs 31:31

For boo-boos, there was Mercurochrome, a Band-Aid, and a kiss. For an upset tummy, there was ginger ale with Ritz crackers, and a sickbed made up on the couch. For fever, there was the test kiss on the forehead, and baby Bayer, and a cool rag. For sunburn or heat rash, there was calamine lotion and a clean bedsheet on Dad's recliner. For the persistent cough in the middle of the night, there was a bite of buttered bread, crusts off. For rainy-day blues, there was tomato soup with pepper and a pat of butter on top. For hurts too deep to name, there was simply quiet abiding, with a hug, as long as need be.

What were your mom's home remedies? Describe her healing properties.

How accurate were her diagnostic skills?

Is there anything expired or recalled in her medicine cabinet?

A mom's hug lasts long after she lets go.

—Unknown

In the family photo album is a picture of my brother, smiling but wan, his feet soaking in a pan of water, on the night he went to the hospital and had emergency surgery. Only recently has it occurred to me to wonder whether she took that photo to help him be cheerful or because she was afraid she wouldn't get another chance to take a picture.

What are some unusual moments your mother documented?

What are her strengths in times of stress?

How did she care for you when you were at your sickest?

Being a mother is learning about strengths you didn't know you had, and dealing with fears you didn't know existed.

—Linda Wooten

She got so mad at me one December during the teen years that she told me she was withholding one of my Christmas presents. Some time after Christmas, in a moment of materialism masked as contrition, I asked about it. It was a leather purse, stamped and embossed with hand-painted flowers, and it had appeared after all, swaddled in white tissue paper in a box under the tree.

When was a time you tried your mother's patience?

Has she bestowed a gift you know you didn't deserve?

How else have you felt her forgiveness?

Some are kissing mothers and some are scolding mothers, but it is love just the same; and most mothers kiss and scold together.

—Pearl S. Buck

She dealt justly but gently and mercifully with me the time I yelled a cuss word in the basement, not knowing how sound traveled through the ductwork; and also the time I called one of my fifth grade classmates a rude name; and also the time I got inexplicably boisterous on the field trip bus when she was a chaperone.

How often did you give your mother cause to be a disciplinarian?

How did she show her wisdom?

Has there been a time that her mercy stunned you more than a deserved punishment would have?

Her mouth is full of wisdom;
kindly teaching is on her tongue.
—Proverbs 31:26

I learned from Mom to respect books by not dog-earing their pages; to respect children by holding conversations with them; and to respect the person I would be tomorrow by always washing today's dishes before going to bed.

How did you witness your mother's respect in action?

How have you shown her your respect?

What's a memorable conversation from your childhood?

Strength and honor are her clothing;
she is confident about the future.

—Proverbs 31:25

PLAYFUL MOM

She teases. She gives nicknames. She's a formidable opponent at Trivial Pursuit. She has some quirky ways of making holidays festive. And she might even have some really surprising sides that you haven't seen, but only heard tell about. In these moments, Mom's still teaching—that there is a time for mirth and a time to play.

One of Mom's family jokes (which the whole family played) involved getting me to believe something and then letting me know I'd been fooled, with the punch line, "And dogs run on batteries."

What's one of your mother's family jokes?

Has she found a gullible nature endearing in you?

How has she shown affection through teasing?

The best way to keep children home is to make the home atmosphere pleasant—and let the air out of the tires. —Dorothy Parker

The board games in heaviest rotation were Yahtzee, Parcheesi, Monopoly, and Trivial Pursuit—mostly games that both required some skill and involved some chance. In Trivial Pursuit, she was especially good at the Literature, and Science and Nature categories.

What games does your mother like to play?

Is she competitive, and how does that manifest itself?

Did she ever let you win, or did she respect you enough to make you work for it?

Every beetle is a gazelle in the eyes of its mother.

—Moorish proverb

We campers would have seen her smiling face dishing up food as we went through the church camp cafeteria line, but the other cooks saw another side of her, like the morning she led them in turning the leftover pancakes into Frisbees and trying to stick them to the walls.

Has your mother ever turned volunteer work into play?

When did you first see a mirthful side to her, or a side that surprised you somehow?

Has she participated in or instigated a food fight at home?

My mother had a great deal of trouble with me, but I think she enjoyed it.

—Mark Twain

Mom was sparing but inventive with nicknames. Sometimes called me Esmerelda Sue, and sometimes Laura Bumbara. She called my brother her 'Possum, for his pretending to be asleep as she would try to wake him from a sofa nap with a kiss on the cheek. At craft fairs we loved the work of a weaver named Tinka, and privately Mom nicknamed her broad-shouldered husband Tonka.

What nicknames or pet names has your mother had for you and your family members?

How did they make you feel?

What nicknames have you had for her?

Women know the way to rear up children (to be just). They know a simple, merry, tender knack of tying sashes, fitting baby-shoes, and stringing pretty words that make no sense. And kissing full sense into empty words. —Elizabeth Barrett Browning

She had the skill of a spy in hiding Easter baskets, even the time my brother's contained a basketball, and she was resistant to play the "warmer, colder" game, preferring to make us look with curiosity and boldness.

What holiday rituals did your mother relish?

Where was the best place she ever hid your Easter basket?

Did she encourage you to find things out for yourself?

The future destiny of a child is always the work of the mother.

—Napoleon Bonaparte

One Halloween when I was sick, she trick-or-treated for me at the homes of the nearest neighbors; another Halloween she dressed up to answer the door and silently handed out candy enshrouded in my red Sears rib cord bedspread and a cheap devil mask; and throughout the year, she would use my brother's astronaut mask, which had a pane of transparent plastic instead of nose and eye holes, when she was cutting onions.

What kind of candy did your household give out on Halloween?

What costumes (for you or herself) did your mom assemble?

Did she find practical uses for them at other times of the year?

The strength of motherhood is greater than natural laws.

—Barbara Kingsolver

She loved being driven to weekend matinees by my brother or me, or both, and she so prized theater naps that after the first time, we were always instructed not to wake her if she fell asleep, which is why she sat through *The Empire Strikes Back* without ever seeing Yoda.

What movies do you remember watching with your mother?

What place have movies had in family fun?

Where is her favorite place to nap?

It is finished. No more training you require. —Yoda

Her favorite actors were Martin Sheen, the British actor Alan Bates, and early Nicolas Cage. I don't know what actresses she admired, but in a movie of her life, I would cast a younger Amy Madigan, for her quiet intensity and for her slightly sharp-edged everyday beauty.

Who are your mom's favorite actors and actresses?

Why?

Who would play her in the movie?

A printed card means nothing except that you are too lazy to write to the woman who has done more for you than anyone in the world. And candy! You take a box to Mother—and then eat most of it yourself. A pretty sentiment. —Anna Jarvis, promoter of the establishment of Mother's Day

She loved well-made handcrafted things and warmed her home with pottery, hand-loomed rugs, a Shaker box, all bought at one or another of the arts and crafts festivals we went to each year, purchases she often followed by saying, "This will be yours when I kick off."

What decorative or utilitarian objects does your mother prize?

What handmade objects does she especially appreciate?

Does she ever, jokingly or seriously, refer to her own death or talk about life after death?

Mothers hold their children's hands for a short while, but their hearts forever.

—Anonymous

EDUCATIONAL MOM

She's your first and longest tenured teacher, and her role involves a lot more than helping with homework. In some ways, every mom is a homeschooler. She's teaching even when it isn't overt—and she's still learning, too.

Even before Mom worked as a bank teller, she was particular about arranging money and taught me to carry my bills the same way she handed them out at her bank window: not only in denominational order—ones, fives, tens, twenties—but also all facing forward with their heads right side up.

What did your mother teach you about money?

What kinds of organizing was she fastidious about? Money? Books? Spices? Kitchenware? Craft items?

What else could you tell about her from looking in her wallet?

Mother—that was the bank where
we deposited all our hurts and worries.
—T. DeWitt Talmage

Mom didn't go to college, but she stayed well informed on general knowledge and current events, partly through the pages of the weekly magazines that came to our house *(Time, Newsweek,* and *The New Yorker,* by subscription, and *People,* bought at the grocery checkout).

Where does your mother get her news? What periodicals do you remember her reading?

When she's curled up with a book, what is it likely to be?

What are nonacademic sources of her smarts?

You may have tangible wealth untold;
Caskets of jewels and coffers of gold.
Richer than I you can never be—
I had a mother who read to me.
—Strickland Gillilan

When we went to the museum and saw a man lingering near the entrance, I thought he was waiting for someone, but after we rounded a corner, Mom said he was waiting until we passed to see whether there was anything left in that pop can on the ledge. I peeked. She was right; he was draining it. It's hard to say which was more remarkable: her powers of observation (I hadn't even noticed the pop can), or her lack of moral judgment about his action.

What did your mother notice about people?

How did one of her predictions come true?

Describe a time your mom was respectful of someone you were ready to be judgmental about.

Most mothers are instinctive philosophers.

—Harriet Beecher Stowe

She liked game shows that required questioning and collaboration (*What's My Line, To Tell the Truth, Password, The $50,000 Pyramid*); series with ensemble casts (*The Waltons; Lou Grant; Hill Street Blues; L.A. Law*); and shows with writerly characters (*My World and Welcome to It; Murder, She Wrote*).

What are your mom's favorite TV shows, now and in the past?

Does she talk back to the TV or shout out the answers?

If her life were a TV show, what kind of show would it be?

No matter how old a mother is, she watches her middle-aged children for signs of improvement.

—Florida Scott-Maxwell

Mom told me once that she worried I would move far away and hardly come home, and I said, "I will not, Mom!" in that exasperated way of know-it-all twenty-somethings who have no idea what the future holds and a dim understanding of their own tendencies and inconsistencies and a dimmer grasp of how much change is beyond our control. When I applied to five graduate schools and my fifth choice was the only one to accept me, I see now it was a blessing, because it was the one closest to home in what turned out to be the last years of her life.

What worries or fears did your mother express to you?

When did a disappointing circumstance turn out to be a blessing in your relationship with your mother?

What know-it-all utterances would you like to apologize to your mother for?

One of the oldest human needs is having someone to wonder where you are when you don't come home at night.

—Margaret Mead

That time at the diner after church, when I blew my straw paper toward Mom, and it was so aerodynamically perfect that it sailed past her and into the back of the teased hairdo of Doris, my Sunday school teacher, Mom quickly conveyed (with one of those Mom looks, to me) that I had done a horrifying, ill-mannered thing, and (with her words, to Doris) that apologies should be swift, and gracious, and leavened with a touch of humor, and that families stick together and forgive without condoning.

When have you embarrassed yourself in front of your mother?

How has she bailed you out?

Put into words something that her silent laser look has said.

There is only one pretty child in the world, and every mother has it. —Chinese proverb

Mom: The Final Exam

No need to remind us to study, Mom: We've
been preparing for this test all our lives.
Grades will not be recorded. Everyone passes.

FILL IN THE BLANKS

It made me feel loved when you

It made me feel safe when you

It made me feel God's presence when you

It made me feel smart when you

It made me feel sad when you

It made me feel proud to be yours when you

It made me feel silly when you

It made me feel good when you

It made me feel God's forgiveness when you

It made me feel big when you

It made me feel like a little kid again when you

A good mother is worth hundreds of schoolmasters.

—George Herbert

SHORT ANSWER

1. If you could go back and change one day with your mom, which one would it be, and why?

2. If you could go back and relive one day with Mom, exactly as it was, which one would it be, and why?

3. If you could give her one perfect day now, what would it have in it?

The mother's heart is the child's schoolroom.
—Henry Ward Beecher

ESSAY QUESTION

Remember when Mom taught you how to write a thank-you note (promptly, saying thank you, naming the gift given, and telling how you will use it or why you appreciate it or why it was a just-right choice)? Write your mother a thank-you note now.

I hope they're still making women like my momma. She always told me to do the right thing. She always told me to have pride in myself; she said a good name is better than money.

—Joe Louis

POSTLUDE

The catalyst for this book was a collection of memories I wrote about my mother. She was fifty years old when she died, and as I approached that age, she was much on my mind. Memories of her were flooding back, and I wanted to preserve them, mostly for myself, to collect in one place all the things that she was to me. Those memories wouldn't submit to being arranged in a narrative, so the resulting essay, "Fifty Things about My Mother," is truly a collection—fifty single sentences, unconnected to the next, but taken together, giving a picture of who she was.

A few of those memories found their way into this book. Readers interested in that essay, or in other things I've written, may find more on my website, lauralynnbrown.com.

I'm interested in where this little book goes and what kinds of stories and familial joys it generates. If you'd like to toss me back a bloom, there's a page on the site for that too. Blessings on all your bouquets of memory, given and received.

BOUQUETS

Thanks to my mother, Linda Lee Gosney Brown, for being a memorable woman, and for caring about words and teaching, in word and deed, to be a good steward of them; to Dad, for marrying her; to Abingdon Press for sowing the seed of this book, and letting me cultivate it, and caring for it all along the way; to Milkglass Creative for designing a just-right cover; to the late Linette Martin, for her example in naming this page; to all the assemblages I call family, biological and otherwise, especially the Central Church lunch bunch and the men and women of Hope House, for support and encouragement and love, and for the gift of seeing me; to everyone who nurtured this work through the fellowship of the table (whether classroom or cafeteria) at The Glen workshops; to Debbie Wright, for asking good questions; to Cynthia Wills, for surrogate sisterhood; to Laura Lapins Willis, for being the pivotal one degree of separation; to Lauren Winner, for well-placed and encouraging words; and to Lil Copan, for her guidance and keenness in bookish matters on and off the page.

My deepest, most indebted gratitude to Jo Lynne and Megan,

the two women besides my mother who have given me the richest appreciation of what it means to be one; and to my brother, Chris, for sharing Mom then and bearing her image now.